USING INSULIN

BY HARRIET BRUNDLE

KidHaven
PUBLISHING

HUMAN BODY HELPERS

Published in 2021 by
KidHaven Publishing, an Imprint of Greenhaven Publishing, LLC
353 3rd Avenue
Suite 255
New York, NY 10010

Edited by: John Wood
Designed by: Danielle Jones

Cataloging-in-Publication Data

Names: Brundle, Harriet.
Title: Using insulin / Harriet Brundle.
Description: New York : KidHaven Publishing, 2021. | Series: Human body helpers | Includes glossary and index.
Identifiers: ISBN 9781534535480 (pbk.) | ISBN 9781534535503 (library bound) | ISBN 9781534535497 (6 pack) | ISBN 9781534535510 (ebook)
Subjects: LCSH: Insulin--Juvenile literature. | Diabetes--Juvenile literature. | Insulin--Therapeutic use--Juvenile literature.
Classification: LCC QP572.I5 B78 2021 | DDC 616.4'62--dc23

Printed in the United States of America

CPSIA compliance information: Batch #BS20K: For further information contact Greenhaven Publishing LLC, New York, New York at 1-844-317-7404.

Please visit our website, www.greenhavenpublishing.com. For a free color catalog of all our high-quality books, call toll free 1-844-317-7404 or fax 1-844-317-7405.

Find us on

IMAGE CREDITS

All images are courtesy of Shutterstock.com, unless otherwise specified. With thanks to Getty Images, Thinkstock Photo, and iStockphoto.
Front Cover & throughout – Beatriz Gascon J, NikaMooni. 2 – Laralova. 5 – metamorworks. 6 – Inspiring, anitnov, Katy Flaty. 7 – Laralova.
8 – PixMarket. 12 – JK's Design. 13 – Irina Qiwi, Victor Z. 17 – DreamLine. 18 – JK's Design.

CONTENTS

Words that look like **this** can be found in the glossary on page 24.

WHAT IS THE PANCREAS?

The pancreas is an <u>organ</u> in your body.

Your pancreas is a part of your digestive system. The digestive system breaks down and takes in the food you eat.

Hi! My name is Polly, and I'm your pancreas.

Your pancreas has some very important jobs. One of its jobs is to make **hormones** called insulin and glucagon. Together, these hormones make sure we have the right amount of glucose, or sugar, in our blood.

I send out hormones into the blood going around your body.

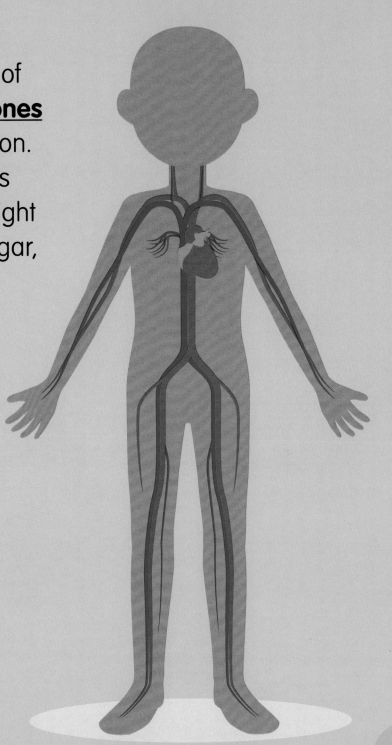

WHAT IS GLUCOSE?

Glucose is a kind of sugar that we get from the things we eat, such as bread, pasta, fruits, and vegetables. Our bodies need glucose for energy.

Some types of food have more sugar than others.

When you eat, your pancreas starts **releasing** insulin. Insulin tells your body to take in the glucose from your food. Your pancreas makes sure you have the right amount of glucose in your blood all the time.

The amount of glucose in your blood is often called your blood sugar level.

SUGAR

WHAT IS DIABETES?

Diabetes is a disease that you get when your blood sugar levels are too high. If your blood sugar levels are too high for a long time, it can be bad for your health.

There are two different types of diabetes: type 1 and type 2.

Blood Sugar Levels

If you have type 1 diabetes, your body doesn't make any insulin at all. With type 2 diabetes, your pancreas is not making enough insulin or the insulin being made isn't doing its job.

HOW DO I KNOW IF I'VE GOT DIABETES?

There are lots of **symptoms** of diabetes. You might feel very thirsty all the time, find you need to urinate, or pee, more often, or feel very hungry even when you've just eaten.

You might feel very tired too.

If you have any of these symptoms, or anything else is making you feel unwell, it's really important that you tell an adult. You might need to be checked by a doctor.

VISITING THE DOCTOR

Your doctor will need to do some tests to find out if you have diabetes. They might want to take some blood from you to check your blood sugar levels.

They might want to check your urine (pee) too.

If the doctor thinks you have diabetes, you might need to go to the hospital for more tests. If you do have diabetes, doctors and nurses can show you how to manage it.

HOW DO I MANAGE MY DIABETES?

Hi, I'm Polly Pancreas. What's your name?

If you have diabetes, you may need to start **injecting** your body with the insulin it should be getting from your pancreas. You might need to take other medicine too.

The doctor will decide what type of insulin you need to take and how much you need. You'll then be shown how to inject yourself safely.

HOW DO I
INJECT INSULIN?

Wash your hands before you start. Prepare your needle, and make sure you've got the right **dose** of insulin. Make sure the skin you're injecting is clean and dry, too.

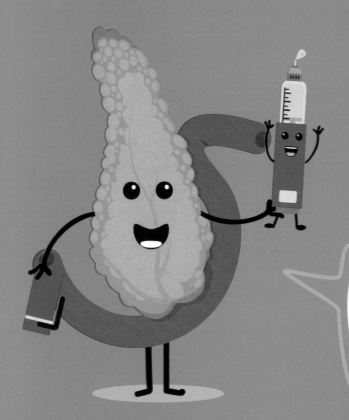

First, you might need to point the needle upward and press the flat end until the insulin appears.

You need to choose a fatty area to inject where you haven't injected recently. Push the needle into your skin, and push down the top until the right amount of insulin has gone into your body.

NEEDLE BIN

Make sure you always get rid of your needles safely.

HOW DO I TEST MY BLOOD SUGAR?

If you have diabetes, it's important that you **<u>regularly</u>** check your blood sugar levels to make sure they are within a healthy range. To do so, most people use a blood glucose meter.

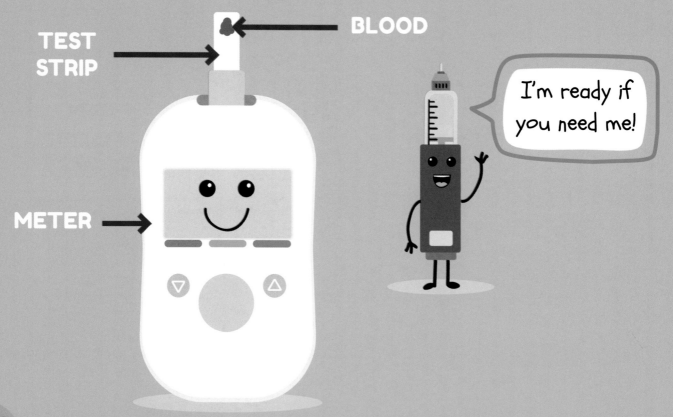

TEST STRIP

BLOOD

METER

I'm ready if you need me!

To use a meter, you need to prick the end of your finger to draw blood. Once you have a drop of blood on your fingertip, you can wipe it on a test strip and your meter tells you the result.

You'll need to put a new test strip into your meter each time you use it.

DOS AND DON'TS

DON'T let your blood sugar level become too low. If this happens, you might feel shaky, sweaty, or have a headache.

DO try to eat a healthy and balanced **diet**.

DO try to inject into a different place each time. It could be on your stomach, thigh, or arm.

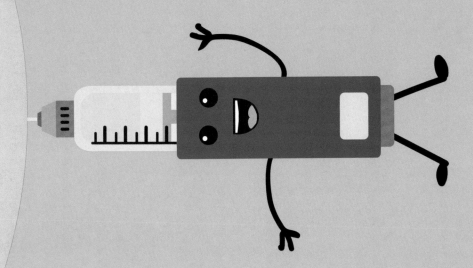

DON'T let your blood sugar level get too high.

LIFE WITH DIABETES

Anyone with type 1 diabetes will have it for the rest of their life. With the use of insulin and a healthy lifestyle, type 1 diabetes can be kept under control.

Thanks, Ian. You're so helpful!

For some people with type 2 diabetes, a change in diet and exercise can **reverse** the disease. This means they no longer need to take any medicine.

GLOSSARY

DIET	the kinds of food you eat
DOSE	an amount of medicine
HORMONES	things that usually travel in the blood and control something in your body
INJECTING	the act of putting something into your body, such as a medicine, using a needle
ORGAN	a part of your body that has a particular job to do
REGULARLY	in an even, fixed pattern
RELEASING	letting go of something
REVERSE	put back to how it was before
SYMPTOMS	the signs of an illness

INDEX